The Aye-Aye

by Jody Rake

Consulting Editor: Gail Saunders-Smith, PhD

Consultant: Dr. Tim Wright
Aye-Aye EEP Coordinator and International Studbook Holder
Durrell Wildlife Conservation Trust
Channel Islands, United Kingdom

Capstone press®

Mankato, Minnesota

Pebble Plus is published by Capstone Press,
151 Good Counsel Drive, P.O. Box 669, Mankato, Minnesota 56002.
www.capstonepress.com

1 2 3 4 5 6 13 12 11 10 09 08

Library of Congress Cataloging-in-Publication Data
Rake, Jody Sullivan.
  The aye-aye / by Jody Rake.
    p. cm. — (Pebble Plus. Weird animals)
  Includes bibliographical references and index.
  Summary: "Simple text and photos describe the homes,
bodies, behaviors, and adaptations of aye-ayes and discusses
ways to protect them" — Provided by publisher.
    ISBN-13: 978-1-4296-1737-6 (hardcover)
    ISBN-10: 1-4296-1737-3 (hardcover)
    1. Aye-aye — Juvenile literature. I. Title. II. Series.
QL737.P935R35 2009
599.8'3 — dc22   2008003899

Editorial Credits
Jenny Marks, editor; Ted Williams and Kyle Grenz, designers, Wanda Winch, photo researcher

Photo Credits
Alamy/A & J Visage, 9, 17,
Bruce Coleman Inc./Norman Myers, 11,
Getty Images Inc./Minden Pictures/Konrad Wothe, 4–5; Minden Pictures/Pete Oxford, 15;
    Oxford Scientific/Photolibrary, 12–13,
Minden Pictures/Frans Lanting, 1, 7, 19, 20–21
Nature Picture Library/Lynn M. Stone, cover

Note to Parents and Teachers

The Weird Animals set supports national science standards related to life science.
This book describes and illustrates aye-ayes. The images support early readers in
understanding the text. The repetition of words and phrases helps early readers learn
new words. This book also introduces early readers to subject-specific vocabulary words,
which are defined in the Glossary section. Early readers may need assistance to read
some words and to use the Table of Contents, Glossary, Read More, Internet Sites, and
Index sections of the book.

Table of Contents

Very Odd Lemurs

Do you see those big eyes peeking through the leaves? They belong to a kind of lemur called an aye-aye.

Aye-ayes live in the forests of Madagascar. Their strange bodies make it easy to live in the treetops.

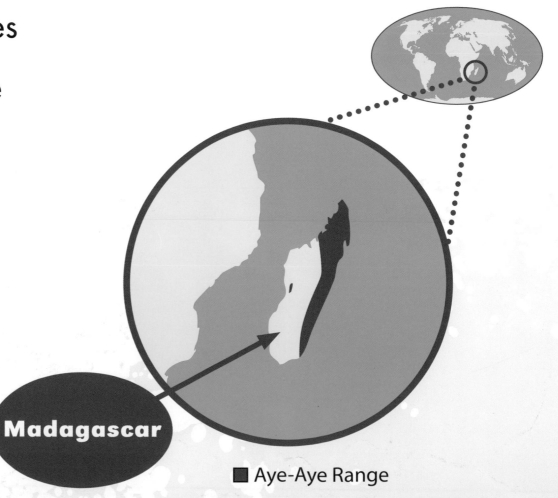

Madagascar

■ Aye-Aye Range

Living in the Trees

Aye-ayes scamper

from tree to tree.

Their long tails help them

balance on branches.

Aye-ayes sleep
in nests all day.
They build their nests
with leaves and branches.

Aye-ayes search
for food at night.
Their big eyes
help them see
in the dark.

13

Finding Food

Aye-ayes hunt for grubs.

They tap on branches

with their long middle fingers.

They listen for grub sounds

with their big ears.

Aye-ayes' sharp teeth
chew through wood.
Their thin middle fingers
dig grubs out of branches.

Life of an Aye-Aye

Aye-ayes are perfect

for living in trees.

But their forests

are being cut down.

Only a few aye-ayes are left.

Aye-ayes are weird
and wonderful.
Protecting their homes
will help save them.

ears
big ears listen for
grub sounds

eyes
large eyes see well
in the dark

fingers
long, skinny fingers
dig for grubs

Glossary

balance — the ability to stay stable and steady

grub — a young insect; aye-ayes eat grubs.

lemur — a kind of primate that lives in trees in Madagascar

Madagascar — a large island nation off the east coast of Africa; aye-ayes are only found in Madagascar.

protect — to guard or keep safe

scamper — to run with short, quick steps

Read More

Gerstein, Sherry. *Animal Planet: The Most Extreme Animals.*
San Francisco: Jossey-Bass, 2007.

Martin, Patricia A. Fink. *Lemurs, Lorises, and Other Lower Primates.*
A True Book. New York: Children's Press, 2000.

Internet Sites

FactHound offers a safe, fun way to find Internet sites related to this book. All of the sites on FactHound have been researched by our staff.

Here's how:

1. Visit *www.facthound.com*

2. Choose your grade level.

3. Type in this book ID **1429617373** for age-appropriate sites. You may also browse subjects by clicking on letters, or by clicking on pictures and words.

4. Click on the **Fetch It** button.

FactHound will fetch the best sites for you!

Index

Word Count: 150

Grade: 1

Early-Intervention Level: 20